Plumed Serpent

Ancient Bearded Gods Of The Americas

Brien Foerster 2016

Cover art by Marcia K. Moore

Contemporary depiction of Quetzalcoatl

Dedication

To those that came before, I salute and thank you for protecting this amazing ancient knowledge under threat and oppression by those that would like to extinguish it. Blessings to modern day wisdom keepers for carrying this information and wisdom in your hearts and minds. And deep thanks, gratitude and love to my dear Irene for being with me through this adventure.

Chapters

1/ Introduction

2/ The Plumed Serpent

3/ Viracocha and Tunupa

4/ Naylamp

5/ Bochica

6/ Gucumatz

7/ Votan

8/ Itzamna

9/ Kukulkan

10/ Quetzalcoatl

11/ Pahana and Awanyu

12/ Bibliography

1/ Introduction

Based on 16th-century accounts of the Spanish conquistadors being "greeted as gods" by the peoples of the New World, certain modern authors have expanded the concept beyond what is historically verifiable, spreading it to the genre of pseudo archaeological literature and fringe theorists, such as writers on ancient astronauts or Atlantis, in some instances (such as Christian Identity) even acquiring quasi-religious or racialist (white supremacist) connotations.

It is claimed by some authors that white missionaries or "gods" visited America before Christopher Columbus. Authors usually quote from mythology and legends which discuss ancient gods such as the Mexican Aztec's Quetzalcoatl to conclude that the legends were actually based on Caucasians, such as Hernan Cortez visiting those areas, and that the Caucasians were really the gods. (1) Spanish chroniclers from the 16th century claimed that when the conquistadors led by Francisco Pizarro first encountered the Inca they were greeted as gods, "Viracochas", because their lighter skin resembled their God Viracocha. This story was first reported by Pedro Cieza de León (1553) and later by Pedro Sarmiento de Gamboa. Similar accounts by Spanish chroniclers (e.g. Juan de Betanzos) describe Viracocha of ancient Bolivia and Peru as a "White God", often with a beard. However, whether the Inca in fact believed this, or the story was simply made up by the Spanish themselves is uncertain. And it could very well be the case as well with Cortez. (2) Writer

Rupert Furneaux also linked "white gods" to the ancient city of Tiahuanaco on the altiplano of Bolivia (3), believed by most academics to be a maximum of 2000 years old, and created by the Tiwanaku culture. However, the author of this book, as well as many geologists and engineers believe it to be far older, and not the work of such local bronze age people.

Depiction of Viracocha on the Sun Gate of Tiwanaku

Colonel A. Braghine in his 1940 book The Shadow of Atlantis claimed that the Carib of the Caribbean Sea area people have reports and legends of a white bearded man who they called Tamu or Zune who had come from the East and taught the people agriculture. He is said to have later disappeared in an "easterly direction." Braghine also claimed that Manco Capac, founder of the Inca civilization in Cusco was a white bearded man. (4) The archaeologist Pierre Honoré in 1962 proposed the fringe theory that the pre-Columbian Mesoamerican civilizations were due to "white men from the vicinity of Crete", while writer Robert F. Marx, who has written extensively about the concept of "White gods", came to the conclusion that white gods "figure in almost every indigenous culture in the Americas." (5)

British writer Harold T. Wilkins took the concept of the white gods the furthest, writing that a vanished white race had occupied the whole of South America in ancient times. Wilkins also claimed that Quetzalcoatl was from Atlantis. (6) And the occultist James H. Madole influenced by Aryanism and Hinduism wrote that the Aryan race was of great antiquity and had been worshipped worldwide by lower races as "white gods". Madole also wrote that the Aryans originated in the Garden of Eden located in North America. (7)

Some Mormons believe that the Aztec deity Quetzalcoatl, a figure sometimes described as white and bearded, who they say came from the sky and promised to return, was likely Jesus Christ. According to the scriptural account recorded in the Book of Mormon, Jesus Christ visited and taught natives of the Americas following his resurrection, and regarded them as the "other sheep," he had referenced during his mortal ministry. The Book of Mormon also claims that Jesus Christ appeared to others, following his resurrection, even to the inhabitants on the "isles of the sea." This latter reference, may offer additional consideration of certain Polynesian accounts. (8)

Ancient bearded ceramic in the Mexico national museum

And finally, some "Ancient astronaut" and UFO writers have claimed the "white gods" were actually extraterrestrials. Peter Kolosimo believed that the legends of Quetzalcoatl had a basis in fact. He claimed that the legends actually describe a race of white men who were born in spaceships and migrated to

Atlantis; then, after Atlantis was destroyed, they moved to the Americas to be treated as "white gods" by the "primitive earth-dwellers". (9)

It is in no way, shape or form the purpose of this book to support racist concepts that Caucasians specifically arrived prior to the savage conquests of Columbus, Cortes, Pizarro and others and supposedly educated the local populations that were encountered. The "white god" and "white skin" terms may refer to people that arrived from distant lands and had skin tones lighter than the resident populations, but the idea that they were necessarily Caucasians has presumably no foundation in actual history.

What is intriguing is that there are so many oral traditions, especially those of South and Central America, as well as Mexico (which is technically part of North America) that describe foreign visitors arriving bearing light skin, often reddish or even blonde hair, and beards. The latter is curious because most Native men of the Americas genetically have little to no facial hair, and many accounts of these foreign visitors stress them having full beards.

Rather than trying to account for all of the oral traditions in the Americas where accounts of foreign visitors in pre-Colombian times with physical characteristics quite unlike those of the local populations occur and where, this book will focus on a relatively small geographical area. Due to the author's main area of expertise being that of the ancient people of what we now call Peru and Bolivia, the story of ancient visitation begins in the Lake Titicaca area, which Peru and Bolivia share. These two nations, and especially Peru had likely the largest populations of people prior to the Spanish arrival, and boasted many great civilizations of which the Inca were the last, and perhaps largest.

Areas to the south and east, such as present day Chile, Argentina, Paraguay and Uruguay likely had smaller populations than those of Peru and Bolivia, as we do not find much in the way of large ancient population centers there. And the Amazonian basin of Brazil may have had numerous people at one time, but true knowledge of this awaits further archaeological studies as, unfortunately, the vast swaths of rain forest are denuded in the 21st century.

Drawing of Quetzalcoatl

2/ The Plumed Serpent

Aztec temple reconstruction; Mexico national museum

The Plumed or Feathered Serpent was a prominent supernatural entity or deity, found in many Mesoamerican religions. It or he was called Viracocha in the Inca and earlier cultures of Peru and Bolivia, Quetzalcoatl among the Aztecs, Kukulkan by the Yucatec Maya, and Gucumatz and Tohil among the K'iche' Maya, for example. The double symbolism used in its name is considered allegoric to the dual nature of the deity or person, where being feathered represents its divine nature or ability to fly to reach the skies and being a serpent represents its human nature or ability to creep on the ground among other animals of the Earth, a dualism very common in Mesoamerican deities. (10)

Monument 19 from La Venta

The earliest conventionally dated representations of feathered serpents appear in the Olmec culture of present day Mexico (circa 1400-400 BC). (11) Most surviving representations in Olmec art, such as Monument 19 at La Venta (above) and a painting in the Juxtlahuaca cave show it as a crested rattlesnake, sometimes with feathers covering the body, and often in close proximity to humans. It is believed that Olmec supernatural entities such as the feathered serpent were the forerunners of many later Mesoamerican deities, (12) although some western experts disagree on the feathered serpent's importance to the Olmec. Oral traditions are unknown as the Olmec apparently died out or were absorbed into the Maya culture at some point. The author explored most of the important and lesser important Olmec sites and museums in February of 2016 and saw very little artistic evidence of the feathered serpent. Thus, it may not have had anything to do with the Olmec civilization, but is very prominent in Aztec, Toltec and Maya art. Should this be the case, then perhaps we can date the arrival of the feathered serpent in Mexico.

The pantheon of the people of Teotihuacan (200 BCE – 700 AD) who were supposedly the Nahua, Otomi, and or Totonac ethnic groups also featured a feathered serpent, shown most prominently on the Temple of the Feathered Serpent (dated 150–200 AD). (13) Several feathered serpent representations appear on the building, including full-body profiles and feathered serpent heads. The actual dating of this building has not been fully proven, thus, the heads may have been added by the later Aztecs. And buildings in Tula, the capital of the later Toltecs (950–1150 AD), also featured profiles of feathered serpents. The Aztec (approximately 1250 to 1521 AD) feathered serpent god Quetzalcoatl is known from several Aztec codices such as the Florentine codex, as well as from the records of the Spanish conquistadors.

Many examples of the feathered serpent at Teotihuacan

Quetzalcoatl was a bringer of knowledge, the inventor of books, and associated with the planet Venus. And the corresponding Mayan god Kukulkan was rare in the Classic era Maya civilization. However, in the Popol Vuh, the K'iche' feathered serpent god Tepeu Gucumatz is the creator of the cosmos. (14)

Quetzalcoatl head at Teotihuacan

In his various incarnations, the feathered serpent was worshipped as the god of wind, the god of water and the morning star god. In 1519, the Spanish explorer Hernan Cortes arrived in Mexico about the same time the Aztec had predicted the return of Quetzalcoatl. This is common in the story of the Feathered or Plumed Serpent in many cultures, that he arrived, taught, left and then declared that he would return. Moctezuma II, the Aztec ruler, allegedly believed that Cortes was the "reincarnation" of the Feathered Serpent. Moctezuma thought that Quetzalcoatl had returned to punish his people for misdeeds and thus he did not defend his city against the invaders. (15)

Human emerging from a serpent's head at Tula

However, whether Moctezuma ever said or in fact believed this is unknown.

Montezuma II with full beard. Representing Quetzalcoatl?

As is often the case where oral traditions of indigenous people are recorded by and then rewritten by those that have conquered them, the original meaning is either skewed or in fact made up altogether as a propaganda tool to belittle the descendants of those conquered.

A case in point of this is the false belief that the Inca of South America made human sacrifices of hundreds if not thousands of their own people, or those that lived within their Inca Federation in order to appease their so called "gods" or deities. Such an idea was in fact a cruel tool invented by the early Catholic, as in Jesuit priests in order to psychologically conquer the people of the area. Very few, as in less than 10 Inca sacrificial victims have ever been found by archaeologists as far as the author knows. And the same can likely be said about the Maya and Aztec people, as well as many others.

What does the term Feathered or Plumed Serpent actually mean? What is it trying to describe? As is often the case, oral traditions of indigenous people cannot be interpreted in a literal sense, nor should they be dismissed, as they often are as being made up stories or "folklore."

Inca period child sacrifice

It has and is often the case that western trained academics, especially those in the fields of archaeology and anthropology do not consult with indigenous people as regards how to properly interpret oral traditions, and the concept of the Feathered or Plumed Serpent is likely such a case.

For the Inca people and other cultures of the highlands of Peru and Bolivia, as well as the Peruvian coast there were three animal figures that loomed prominent in their artistic and oral knowledge; the snake, puma and condor. Usually all three would be found together and three was their sacred number whereas four was often the sacred number of other Native American people. As is usually the case, the true meaning of what these animals represented and why there were three rather than another number is far more complex than what most academic books and tour guides will tell you.

Basically, and what you will often hear is that the snake represented, and still represents to some people wisdom, while the puma is a symbol of strength and condor that of spirituality. On another level they represent what are known as the lower, middle and upper worlds, as well as past, present and future. In a deeper way they also mean snake=subconscious mind, puma=conscious mind and condor=superconscious. As the snake in many traditions is known to be an ancient animal and crawls on the ground, it best represents the wisdom of the earth, and overwhelmingly and in various cultures, deals with primordial life force. (16) For the Puma these noble cats are symbols of courage and power, and were interpreted by the Inca and others to be the best symbol of the alert and conscious mind.

Sculpture of Inca, snake, Puma and Condor near Machu Pic'chu

As regards the condor, the Andean condor is a national symbol of Argentina, Bolivia, Chile, Colombia, Ecuador, Peru and Venezuelan Andes states. It is the national bird of Bolivia, Chile,

Colombia, and Ecuador. It plays an important role in the folklore and mythology of the South American Andean regions, and has been represented in Andean art from c. 2500 BC onward. In Andean mythology, the Andean condor was associated with the sun deity, (17) and was believed to be the ruler of the upper world, thus, the spiritual realm.

In Central America and Mexico, the snake symbol is very prevalent, as is the puma (or jaguar depending on the location) and the condor is replaced by the eagle. The current coat of arms of Mexico has been an important symbol of Mexican politics and culture for centuries. The coat of arms depicts a Mexican golden eagle perched on a prickly pear cactus devouring a snake. To the people of Tenochtitlan (Mexico City today) this would have strong religious connotations, but to the Europeans, it would come to symbolize the triumph of good over evil (with the snake sometimes representative of the serpent in the Garden of Eden).

The coat of arms recalls the founding of Mexico City, which again was originally called Tenochtitlan. The legend of Tenochtitlan as shown in the original Mexica codices, paintings, and post-Cortesian codices, does not include a snake. While the Fejérváry-Mayer codex depicts an eagle attacking a snake, other Mexica illustrations, such as the Codex Mendoza, show only an eagle. In the text of the Ramírez Codex, however, Huitzilopochtli (sun and war deity as well as the patron of the city of Tenochtitlan) asked the Tenochtitlan people to look for an eagle devouring a snake, perched on a prickly pear cactus.

Modern Mexican flag

In the text by Chimalpahin Cuauhtlehuanitzin, the eagle is devouring something, but it is not mentioned what it is. Still other versions (such as the backside of the Teocalli of the Sacred War) show the eagle clutching the Aztec symbol of war, the Atl-Tlachinolli glyph, or "burning water". (18)

Moreover, the original meanings of the symbols were different in numerous aspects. The eagle was a representation of the sun god Huitzilopochtli, who was very important, as the Mexicas referred to themselves as the "People of the Sun". The cactus (Opuntia ficus-indica), full of its fruits, called "nochtli" in

Nahuat
Tenoch

Author with a Toltec "feathered serpent warrior" figure at Tula

To the Mexicas, the snake represented wisdom, and it had strong connotations with the god Quetzalcoatl. The story of the snake was derived from an incorrect translation of the Crónica mexicáyotl by Fernando Alvarado Tezozómoc. In the story, the Nahuatl text ihuan cohuatl izomocayan, "the snake hisses", was mistranslated as "the snake is torn". Based on this, Father Diego Durán reinterpreted the legend so that the eagle represents all that is good and right, while the snake represents evil and sin. Despite its inaccuracy, the new legend was adopted because it conformed with European heraldic tradition. To the Europeans it would represent the struggle between good and evil. Although this interpretation does not conform to pre-Columbian traditions, it was an element that could be used by the first missionaries for the purposes of evangelism and the conversion of the native peoples. (19)

The actual interpretation by the author, if we remove all of the twists and turns of Spanish colonial polluted ideas is that the eagle and snake symbol could in fact represent the unity of the snake and condor, as in the merger of the subconscious and super conscious. Tenoch is said to have been an Aztec warrior/ruler who, according to legend, was given a vision in which he saw an eagle atop a cactus plant with a snake in its mouth and thus named the new Aztec capital Tenochtitlan.

Early drawing of Tenochtitlan

However, the author learned during a trip through ancient sites in Mexico in February of 2015 from a local Native guide that Tenoch in fact means prophecy or prophet. Thus, Tenochtitlan would more correctly mean the "place of the prophesy" or "place of the prophets." The act of prophesy is often best achieved through meditation where the conscious mind is cleared so that the subconscious and superconscious aspects of the mind may interact freely. Therefore, using a symbol such as a snake and eagle intertwined could in fact represent a high state of being, rather than the worn out and erroneous "good versus evil" paradigm.

So, it could be that the Plumed/Feathered Serpent concept is one that represents a being, person or people of a very high state of mental consciousness. That the Plumed and Feathered Serpent story is found in various parts of South and Central America as well as Mexico is of course intriguing, especially if the varied groups involved were not in contact with each other. Now we will explore each of the major Plumed Serpent identities, starting in the area of Lake Titicaca in Peru and Bolivia, and progress northwards in to Central America and Mexico, and beyond.

3/ Viracocha and Thunupa

Although the earliest known representations of the Plumed Serpent, according to standard archaeology appear in the Olmec culture as far back as 1400 BC, though many, including the author doubt that, those of the ancient character known as Viracocha or Thunupa could in fact be older. Viracocha is the great creator deity in the pre-Inca and later Inca mythology in the Andes region of South America. His full name and some spelling alternatives are Wiracocha, Apu Qun Tiqsi Wiraqutra, and Con-Tici (also spelled Kon-Tiki, the source of the name of explorer Thor Heyerdahl's raft)

The author with Diana Taylor at Tiwanaku. Viracocha is above our heads

Viracocha. Viracocha was one of the most important deities in the Inca pantheon and seen as the creator of all things, or the substance from which all things are created. (21) Viracocha created the universe, sun, moon, and stars, as well as time (by commanding the sun to move over the sky) and civilization itself. He was worshipped as god of the sun and of storms and was represented as wearing the sun for a crown, with thunderbolts in his hands, and sometimes tears descending from his eyes as rain, such as at Tiwanaku on the southern edge of Lake Titicaca.

According to a myth recorded by Juan de Betanzos, Viracocha rose from Lake Titicaca (or sometimes the cave of Paqariq Tampu (also spelled Paqariqtampu, Pacarictambo and Pacaric Tambo) near Cusco during the time of darkness to bring forth light. (22) This of course was after he is alleged to have created the universe and earth. He made the sun, moon, and the stars, or possible these entities became visible once light had been created. Then he made mankind by breathing into stones, but his first creation were brainless giants that displeased him. So he destroyed it with a flood and made a new, better one from smaller stones, or some sources say from clay. (23) In some accounts it was these brainless giants that assembled the megalithic site known on the high altiplano as Tiwanaku and Puma Punku. If they were rather stupid, then it is likely that Viracocha himself was responsible for the quarrying and shaping of the massive stones themselves.

There exists in Bolivia a legend in which the gods decide to punish a city on the edge of a lake by submerging it in a day of earthquakes and floods. The principal god, Thunupa, also known as Viracocha who had tried to persuade the people to amend their degenerate ways is cast by the people adrift on the lake in a reed boat which is then carried southwards to crash against the southern shores of the lake. (24)

Thunupa carved profile at Ollantaytambo

A great aperture opens up in the side of the lake, carrying the god southwards in a great flood of water until he reaches Lake Poopo where he disappears into the waters in the region of

Pampa Aullagas. Other versions say the waters continued south in a great wave even reaching Chile where a giant petroglyph representing Tunupa can be seen in the Atacama Desert. According to the above version of the legend, the inhabitants of the city shown as Tiwanaku were drowned by the rising waters of Lake Titicaca in the southern part of the lake today known as Winay Marka.

Atacama giant photographed by the author

However, later on this chapter we will see that there was also a person, or people in human form, named Viracochan, who was in fact said to have walked the land. He (or they) was sent by the creator Viracocha to teach the people. Now getting back to Tiwanaku. Bolivian archaeologist Arthur Posnansky thought that Tiwanaku dated as far back as 15,000 BC and that the city had been at one time submerged by the waters of Lake Titicaca due to higher up lakes bursting their banks and pouring water down into Lake Titicaca. His opinion was based upon materials found in excavations at the Kalasasaya in Tiwanaku and his findings are rejected by modern archaeology, but local legends also talk of submerged buildings beneath the lake. Evidence of submerged terraces were found by divers of the Akakor expedition and historically, the levels of the lake have always risen and retracted as a result of climate change. It is possible that an older city awaits discovery beneath Tiwanaku or the nearby lake.

Geologically, Lake Titicaca was known as Lake Tauca from 11,000 to 9,500 BC. At this time the Desaguadero river was horizontal and parallel to the lake level and water would drain from the Salar de Uyuni (to the south) northwards. At some time after lake Tauca in 11,000 BC, the northern end has risen and the southern end has sunk given the slanted ancient shore lines. Water today drains from Lake Titicaca southwards to Lake Poopo and Uyuni. (25) If this happened suddenly, then the water from Lake Titicaca (Tauca) would flow southwards in a giant tidal wave wiping out everything in its path and submerging the island of Atlantis in Lake Poopo. This would put a date of the possibly last appearance of the of the god Viracocha at being prior to 9,500 BC. The man (or people) called Viracochan would have clearly come much later.

Having created humanity after the destruction of the giants, it is said that Viracocha eventually disappeared across the Pacific Ocean (by walking on the water), and never returned. But how can this be possible? An incarnate creator? Again, it is likely that we must make a distinction between Viracocha the creator god and stories of Viracochan; he or those sent by the creator to walk the earth, and eventually disappear by crossing the Pacific Ocean. From this we can possibly get a time line as to when Viracochan appeared in the area.

Evidence of ancient mud flow at the Kalasasaya at Tiwanaku

He, Viracochan wandered the earth disguised as a beggar, teaching the new creations the basics of civilization, as well as working numerous miracles. He wept when he saw the plight of the creatures that Viracocha had created. It was thought that Viracochan would re-appear in times of trouble, and this is the same story that we will see as regards Quetzalcoatl. Pedro Sarmiento de Gamboa wrote that Viracochan was described as "a man of medium height, white and dressed in a white robe secured round the waist, and that he carried a staff and a book in his hands." (26) As de Gamboa was a colonial Spaniard with close ties to the Catholic church it is likely that added in the idea of the book, as in bible as such things were not present in South America prior to the Spanish conquest.

Bust of the god or high Inca Viracocha

The idea that Viracochan was white in skin colour could again be an exaggeration on the part of de Gamboa, like the presence of the book in order to corrupt the original oral traditions as a way of introducing Christian principles to the Native people. In one legend he had one son, Inti (which is the Inca name for the Sun) and two daughters, Mama Killa (the Moon) and

Pachamama (the Earth.) In this legend, he destroyed the people around Lake Titicaca with a Great Flood called Unu Pachakuti, saving two to bring civilization to the rest of the world, these two being Manco Capac, the son of Inti (sometimes taken as the son of Viracocha), which name means "splendid foundation", and Mama Uqllu, which means "mother fertility". However, this was likely a reference to Viracocha and not Viracochan. These two founded the Inca civilization carrying a golden staff, called 'tapac-yauri' to the site of Cusco, which became their capital. In another legend, he fathered the first eight civilized human beings and in some stories, he had a wife called Mama Qucha. In this case the Viracocha referred to could very well be the god or deity, and not the man.

In another legend, Viracochan had two sons, Imahmana Viracocha and Tocapo Viracocha. After the Great Flood and the Creation, or re-creation Viracocha sent his sons to visit the tribes to the northeast and northwest to determine if they still obeyed his commandments. Viracocha himself traveled North. During their journey, Imahmana and Tocapo gave names to all the trees, flowers, fruits, and herbs. They also taught the tribes which of these were edible, which had medicinal properties, and which were poisonous. Eventually, Viracocha, Tocapo and Imahmana arrived at Cusco (in modern-day Peru) and then the Pacific seacoast where they walked across the water until they disappeared. This supposedly occurred at a place called Manta in Ecuador, near the Peru border and since he is said to have walked the land then this would be Viracochan.

Present day Manta in Ecuador

The word Viracocha literally means "sea foam." Some theorize that the term is a description of the fact that when he sailed away, all that he left behind was the wake of his ship, being foam on the sea. In other accounts he is said to have told those that he encountered that he came "from the foam of the sea" possibly referring to the idea that his homeland had sunk and left nothing behind but bubbles or foam from the sinking landmass.

Again, Spanish chroniclers from the 16th century claimed that when the conquistadors led by Francisco Pizarro first encountered the Inca they were greeted as gods, "Viracochas", because their lighter skin resembled their Viracochan. This story was first reported by Pedro Cieza de León (1553) and later by Pedro Sarmiento de Gamboa. Similar accounts by Spanish chroniclers (e.g. Juan de Betanzos) describe Viracocha(n?) as a "White God", often with a beard. (27) The whiteness of Viracocha is however not mentioned in the native authentic legends of the Incas and most modern scholars therefore consider the "White God" story to be post-conquest Spanish invention.

Similar to the Incan god Viracocha, the Aztec god Quetzalcoatl and several other deities from Central and South American pantheons, Bochica of Colombia and Panama is described in legends as being bearded. The beard, once believed to be a mark of a prehistoric European influence and quickly fueled and embellished by spirits of the colonial era, had its single significance in the continentally insular culture of Mesoamerica. The Anales de Cuauhtitlan is a very important early source which is particularly valuable for having been originally written in Nahuatl which describes the attire of Quetzalcoatl at Tula:

"Immediately he made him his green mask; he took red color with which he made the lips russet; he took yellow to make the facade; and he made the fangs; continuing, he made his beard of feathers..." (28)

Bochica monument in Boyaca Colombia

In this quote the beard is represented as a dressing of feathers, fitting comfortably with academic impressions of Mesoamerican art. The local indigenous Andean stories, however, do not mention whether Viracochan had facial hair or not with the point of outfitting him with a mask and symbolic feathered beard being to cover his unsightly appearance because as Viracocha said "If ever my subjects were to see me, they would run away!" (29) While descriptions of Viracochan's physical appearance are open to interpretation, it should be noted that men with beards were frequently depicted by the

Peruvian Moche culture of the north coast in its famous pottery, long before the arrival of the Spanish.

Pre-Colombia Chimu ceramic from Peru showing red beard

Modern advocates of fringe theories however such as a pre-Columbian European migration to Peru continue to cite these bearded ceramics and Viracocha's beard as being evidence for an early presence of a non-Amerindian race in Peru. (30) As the Moche existed between 100 and 800 AD, this gives us a timeline as regards when the above ceramic was created. Should at least some of the ceramics be from the earlier period, it does open up the possibility that Viracochan, Kukulkan and Viracochan was or were the same people. Just a thought for now.

Although most Indians do not have heavy beards, there are groups who do, such as the Aché of Paraguay who also have light skin but who show no evidence of admixture with Europeans and Africans. When the Southern Paiutes (Arizona, southeastern California, Nevada and Utah) were first contacted by Europeans in 1776, the report by fathers Silvestre Vélez de Escalante and Francisco Atanasio Domínguez noted that "Some of the men had thick beards and were thought to look more in appearance like Spanish men than native Americans". (31)

According to local myth, a representation of the messenger of Viracocha ('The Creator of Civilization') named Viracochan, Wiracochan or Tunupa is shown in the small village of Ollantaytambo, southern Peru. Ollantaytambo located in the department of Cusco makes up a chain of small villages along the Urubamba Valley. Also known as the Sacred Valley of the Incas, it was an important stronghold of the Incan Empire. Facing the ancient Inca ruins of Ollantaytambo in the rock face of Cerro Pinkuylluna is the 140-meter-high figure of Viracochan.

The angry looking formation of his face is made up of indentations that form the eyes and mouth, whilst a protruding carved rock denotes the nose. There is also one tooth in his mouth. Inca ruins built on top of the face are also considered to represent a crown on his head. Artists' impressions of the rock face also include a heavy beard and a large sack upon his shoulders. It is unlikely that this was a work of the Inca due to its sheer scale and inaccessibility, so it may be much older.

The Inca likely arose at about 100 AD as a cohesive group in the area of Lake Titicaca, likely on the Island of the Sun and Island of the moon, and did not enter Cusco until about 1000 years later. Thus, it is possible that Viracochan first appeared to them at about this date, and was the driving force that made the Inca such a complex civilization over time. As a human, he unlikely "rose from the waters" of the lake but most likely first established himself there. We will see later that Kukulkan and Quetzalcoatl both first arrive, by many accounts "from the east." It is possible that Viracochan also came from the east, as in the Atlantic Ocean, following the river system of what is now the nation of Paraguay. First he would have entered the Rio de la Plata, then the Parana, and finally either the Pilcomayo (an Inca name by the way) or Bermejo. From there, at the source of one of these two rivers, he could easily cross on the Altiplano, where Lake Titicaca exists.

The Viracochan/Tunupa face at Ollantaytambo

In other accounts, Viracochan, the pilgrim preacher of knowledge, the master knower of time, is described as a person with superhuman power, a tall man, with short hair, dressed like a priest or an astronomer with tunic and a bonnet with four pointed corners. According to travel writer Paul Jones, "This incredible myth of a Viracocha spreads throughout South America and beyond. This ancient mystical God, who by local legend rose from the middle of Lake Titicaca to create mankind was and is still today truly respected. The rock carving at Ollantaytambo is a striking reminder of the spiritual connections the Incas had with the Andes."(32)

Traditional Wari culture hats from the highlands of Peru

The Wari culture, who lived near the area north of Lake Titicaca from 600 to 1000 AD had traditional cornered hats similar to what Viracochan supposedly wore.

As has been previously discussed, the general consensus is that Viracochan (Tunupa) first appears in the Lake Titicaca area and walks to the Pacific Ocean near the present Peru/Ecuador border teaching along the way. It is said that some of the places where he stopped included Cusco, Ollantaytambo, Cajamarca and others along what has been called The Path of Viracocha through the highlands of Bolivia and Peru.

In the 1970s the Dutch-Peruvian mathematician, Maria Sholten D'Ebneth wrote a book in which she claimed to have discovered, or rediscovered, an alignment of pre-Columbian sacred sites stretching from the ancient city of Tiwanaku (Tiahuanaco) in Bolivia to north of the city of Cajamarca in northern Peru. The alignment appeared to be incredibly accurate and covered a distance of around 1,000 miles (1,600 km), cutting across some of the highest mountains and steepest gradients in the entire world. The alignment had a precise orientation of exactly 45° West from true North, following the line of the Andes mountains. (33)

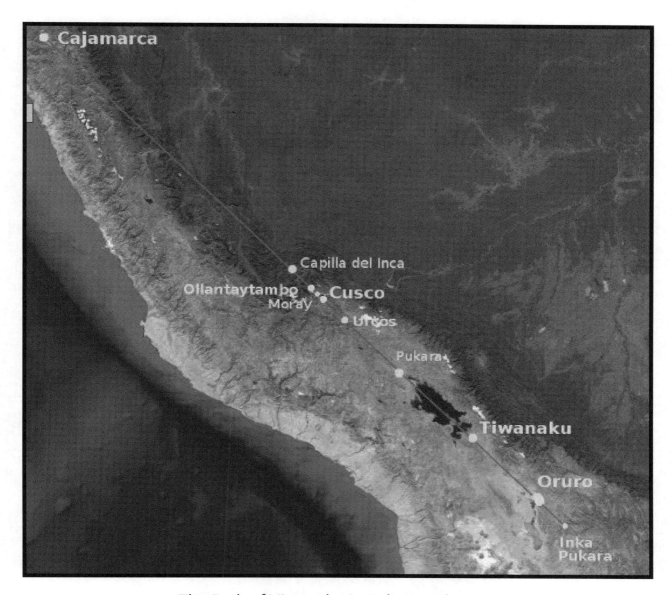

The Path of Viracocha in Bolivia and Peru

Published only in Spanish, and now out of print, Sholten D'Ebneth's, La Ruta de Wiracocha (The Route or Path of Viracocha) (34) contains a wealth of information hardly known to the English speaking world. The alignment's association with Viracochan, the teacher and civilizer of humankind, is a highly significant one. Many legends concerning the feats of Viracocha speak of his undertaking a journey, from the city of Tiwanaku towards the North West, eventually to leave the shores of South America's Pacific coast just south of the present day border between Peru and Ecuador. Viracocha's legendary journey, Sholten D'Ebneth revealed, corresponded with her own geometrical discovery of the alignment of many of the most ancient and sacred sites in the Andes, including the famous ones at Cusco (Cuzco), Ollantaytambo and, of course, the great and mysterious complex of Tiwanaku.

The many megalithic sites along Way of Viracocha have long given rise to theories and speculations about who built them and controversies about when they were built. At this juncture, it is perhaps worth pondering the sheer technical challenge of surveying this vast alignment across some of the most rugged, remote and mountainous terrain on earth. Indeed, the research of Dave Truman and others, indicate that the alignment could extend beyond Tiwanaku. The Peruvian architect Carlos Millena Villena has even suggested that it may form part of a great circle that girdles the entire globe. Whatever the length of the alignment is eventually determined to be, whoever surveyed it must have been aware of the curvature of the earth.

When Truman plotted the Route of Viracocha, he had the benefit of using software such as Google Earth and Marble.

Possible Viracocha statue at Tiwanaku

These programs enabled him to employ a spherical projection of the whole globe, rather than the "flat" Mercator Projection used in previous decades. As we will see later, using this map projection yielded rather different results from those of earlier researchers. This became evident when he extended Sholten D'Ebneth's alignment beyond Tiwanaku towards the South East. If his findings are correct, it implies that whoever surveyed the Path of Viracocha, not only had an understanding of the earth's curvature, but also understood the principles of spherical trigonometry. It is equally likely that those who undertook this work knew the dimensions of the Earth.

Sholten D'Ebneth discovered the connection between the Path of Viracocha and the geometry of an ancient South American sacred symbol, called the chakana. Certain symbols seem to defy the changes brought about by time and ebb and flow of history. In South America, one such symbol is the chakana. Otherwise known as the Andean stepped cross, it has been found in the relics of so many of the varied pre-Columbian cultures of South America. In one form or another, you will find it in the Mapuche art work in Chile, on the enigmatic stone blocks of Puma Punku in Bolivia, on the embroideries of the Incas, adorning the adobe walls of the city of Chan Chan and woven into the textiles of the war-like Huari culture. It has been found in the ancient pyramid city of Caral, which dates to around 4,000 BC, where it embellishes the joists of the Ceremonial Centre. Yet another name for it is the Inca Cross, but its provenance as a symbol is much more ancient. As with other symbols of great antiquity, the multiple meanings associated with chakana are the result of accretions over time.

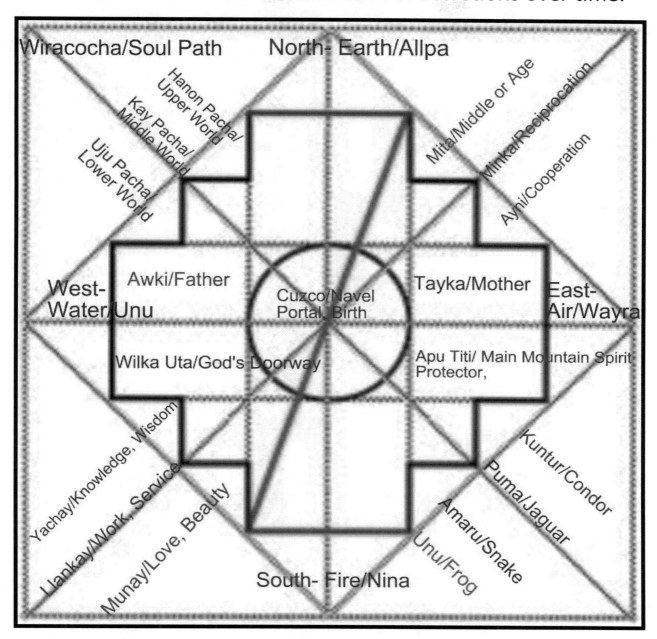

Complex symbolism of the Chakana

In classical Euclidean geometry, this process known as squaring the circle and was a fundamental task set for students of the discipline. In sacred geometry and alchemy, the square and the circle are thought to represent opposite principles; the square being masculine and the circle feminine. However, they are equal in that both consist of 360°. In esoteric terms, the act of squaring the circle equates with the unifying of masculine and feminine principles at work in the universe. Interestingly, a Peruvian researcher into the Route of Viracocha, Javier Lajo, found that many ancient sites and temples along its length had either square or circular geometry, depending on whether they were dedicated to male or female deities. (35)

It is no coincidence that many of the megalithic sites identified by Sholten D'Ebneth along the Path of Viracocha appear to be extremely ancient. Of course, this view is counter to academically trained archaeologists, who see the development of culture in the Andes as a matter of slow and steady progress. In their scenario, none of the megalithic structures are much older than about 500BC (Tiwanaku/Puma Punku), and many of them, which they consider to have been built by the Incas (Cusco, Ollantaytambo), are considered much more recent still. So called alternative theorists such as this author consider these and other megalithic sites in the Andes to be the remains of an extremely ancient advanced culture, or cultures. There is some evidence to support the latter view in the legends of the indigenous peoples of the Andes. Many of these speak of a time in the distant past, when there was a great civilization of demi-gods, called the Ñapac Machula (The Wise Old Ones), (36) elsewhere called the Viracochans.

The author with one of the astonishing stones of Tiwanaku/Puma Punku

They speak of a rush of water that was accompanied by fire raining down on the land from the heavens. All of this occurred when, so the locals say, the sun went dark. Could this account for the time when Viracocha the god destroyed his first creation, the giants? And did the blackening of the sky mean, that once cleared the Sun, Moon and stars were not created, but recreated?

This account is similar to ones of the cataclysmic transitions that took place, both before and after the Younger Dryas period. This was the final and sudden reprise of the Ice Age, lasting from around 10,900 BC to 9,500 BC (37) in what geologists now consider a very turbulent transformation from an extended period of glaciations to the current Holocene era. Was this really an account of those far-off times? If so, it may have immense significance for the dating of this and other sites along the Path of Viracocha. And also curiously, if the Path of Viracocha is extended beyond the area near the Peru/Ecuador border to the we encounter another tradition about an ancient Plumed Serpent character, and bearded once called Bochica.

4/ Naylamp

Modern actor dressed as Naylamp

Following the Path of Viracocha, we are now at the north coast of Peru. The Moche civilization flourished in northern Peru with its capital near present day Moche and Trujillo, from about 100 AD to 800 AD, during what is called the Regional Development Epoch. While this issue is the subject of some debate, many scholars contend that the Moche were not politically organized as a monolithic empire or state. Rather, they were likely a group of autonomous polities that shared a common elite culture, as seen in the rich iconography and monumental architecture that survive today.

There are several theories as to what caused the demise of the Moche political structure. Some scholars have emphasized the role of environmental change. Studies of ice cores drilled from glaciers in the Andes reveal climatic events between 536 to 594 AD, possibly a super El Niño, that resulted in 30 years of intense rain and flooding followed by 30 years of drought, part of the aftermath of the climate changes of 535 to 536.

Once the Moche civilization had collapsed, the people of the region reverted to simple farmers lacking organization or a central focus. The glorious times of monument building were over, and the people were disillusioned with the old religion they represented. Their sacrifices brought them drought and floods, not the stability they had hoped for.

It was into this scene that one day arrived a fleet of small sea-faring vessels from the north, some contend. The lead boat landed on the beach and a man, named Naylamp, dressed in exotic riches stepped ashore. Wearing gold ornaments and an elaborate headdress of hundreds of strange exotic feathers unknown to the region, the man said to have great talent and courage beaconed the other ships to follow.

The local Moche descendants, so impressed with this mysterious man from the ocean, bowed at his feet, one woman offering him food and water. He married this woman and set about organizing the people into a city and eventually a nation state. The Sican/Chimu civilization had begun. Peruvian legends say that the large fleet of rafts led by Naylamp landed near the mouth of the River Faquisllanga, near the modern day city of Lambayeque. They found an ideal place to settle down and build a palace, which they called Chot. At the most notable location of the palace they placed a sculpture carved in green stone, a figure that was supposed to represent Naylamp himself. According to studies, this could have happened, between 900 and 1300 AD.

Many years went by, and Naylamp lived a prosperous life raising many children until he abandons his people, flying off, just like a bird. Today there are several theories that speak of Naylamp and his origins.

Artist rendition of the arrival of Naylamp

José Kimmich, who studied the Chimu origin, published in 1917 a study claiming that Naylamp was of Asian origin offering anthropological, linguistic, paleographic and architectural evidence. To Kimmich both the Chimu and Lambayeque have Indochinese origin and even now coastal indigenous people can easily be mistaken for an Indochinese. Ten centuries ago the Chinese and Indochinese sailed in boats that carried 100 tons and were very sea worthy. It may well be that the craft of Naylamp, reaching the California coast and following the line of the coast south, could have made it to Peru.

There are quite a few researchers who believe that Naylamp was of Maya origin. Among those supporters is archaeologist Max Uhle who based on archaeological evidence supports this theory.

Riva Aguero supported this theory because he claims that a lot of words, names of places and people have similarity to the Mayan and the Aztec Nahuatl languages.

An impressive story. Some say there may even be a connection between the fall of the Maya in Mexico and the rise of the Chimu and Sican, which occurred at the same time. The truth is though, if this was the case, the Maya would have almost certainly brought their written language with them. We do know there was pre-Inca trade with central America, which is why we have corn in Peru, some theorize there were even direct trade links with central America.

There does seem to be some evidence though of a group of people arriving from the north and starting a civilization in the region. Chronicler Cabello de Balboa, in 1586 heard the story from locals in Lambayeque and first told it to the Spanish. Later, famous archaeologist Bruning in the early 1900s indicated that the river Faquisllanga in Lambayeque may have been the arrival point where Naylamp constructed his palaces and temples. In the ancient ruins of these constructions he found an emerald idol (Emeralds are a national export of Colombia).

Researcher Hermann Leicht believes that Naylamp was only one of the many who originated from central America and arrived at the coast of Lambayeque. All of the previously mentioned are certainly very valid theories; but there are alternative theories that are worlds apart. Naylamp is very similar to Quetzalcoatl and Viracocha, two of the most important ancient deities of central and south America. Strangely, just like Quetzalcoatl and Viracocha, Naylamp left his people, in his case flying off and into the sky, promising to return one day.

Gold mask believed to be a portrayal of Naylamp

Some believe that the legend of Naylamp actually speaks of a member of the Anunnaki, who were deities of the ancient Sumerians of the Middle East. It is believed, by ancient astronaut theorists, that Naylamp belonged to the ancient Anunnaki and arrived at the coasts of Peru in search of Gold. Peruvian ancient legends tell the story that Naylamp abandoned his people flying off like a bird. Curiously the Anunnaki figures left by the ancient Sumerians are represented by winged men. However, this is definitely what is referred to as fringe theory, with little or no substantial evidence.

Many ancient astronaut theorists suggest that legends such as that of Naylamp actually speak of the Anunnaki who came to Earth for a specific purpose, leaving behind only legends. It is worth mentioning that ancient cultures for the Americas such as the Maya, Aztec and Olmec, which predate the previous two, were very skillful sculptors, and their main ornaments were made from Jade stone.

The Yampallec figure which is believed to represent Naylamp is also made from jade. As the above photos show, there appear to be no representations or other references to Naylamp as having been bearded. And since he seems to have possibly appeared about a thousand years after the appearance of Viracochan, he may have been a completely different person from a different part of the world.

The correlation between cultures of ancient America such as the Pre-Inca, Inca, Maya, Aztecs and other, who not only share similar customs and traditions, but had very similar knowledge in fields such as astronomy, construction, etc. point toward the possibility that all of them shared a common teacher, one that, according to some legends, came from the stars.

Ceremonial knife called a tumi portraying Naylamp

5/ Bochica

Bochica is a figure in the mythology of the Muisca (Chibcha) culture, which existed before the arrival of the Spanish conquistadores in areas comprising parts of present-day Colombia and Panama. He was the founding hero of their civilization, who according to legend brought morals and laws to the people and taught them agriculture and other crafts. (38) Similarly to the Incan teacher Viracochan, the Aztec's Quetzalcoatl and several other deities from Central and South American pantheons, Bochica is described in legends as being bearded. The beard, once mistaken as a mark of a prehistoric European influence and quickly fueled and embellished by spirits of the colonial era, had its single significance in the continentally insular culture of Mesoamerica. The connotation of the word 'beard' by Spanish colonizers was grossly abused as foundation for embellishment and fabrication of an original European influence in Mesoamerica and thus possibly justification for conquest, as we have seen. And there have been questions on the authenticity of the preserved stories, and to what level they have been corrupted by the beliefs and imagery incorporated by Spanish Christian missionaries and monks who first chronicled the native legends. (39)

According to Chibcha legends, Bochica was a bearded man who came from the east, like Kukulkan, Quetzalcoatl and possibly Viracochan. He taught the primitive Chibcha people ethical and moral norms and gave them a model by which to organize their states, with one spiritual and one secular leader.

Bochica and his followers

Bochica also taught the people agriculture, metalworking and other crafts before leaving for the west to live as an ascetic. When the Chibcha later forsook the teachings of Bochica and turned to a life of excess, a flood engulfed the Savannah of Bogotá, where they lived. Upon appealing for aid from their hero, Bochica returned on a rainbow and with a strike from his staff, created the Tequendama Falls, through which the floodwaters could drain away. (40)

'Many moons ago, during the childhood of humanity when everything was new, the people worshipped many gods, praying for every last thing. And then one day a bearded gray-haired man came to the land of Colombia. He came from the highlands, from a land known as Chingaza in the eastern part of that country, and he had an important message for all the people.

He was a startling sight, tall and fierce looking, weathered and dressed in a tunic. In his strong bronzed hand, he carried a large gold scepter. His name, he told the people, was Bochica, and he wanted the people to learn how to care for themselves. And so he began to teach them. He taught them to sow their fields, and to plant and to harvest them. He taught them how to build houses, and how to weave cotton and other fibers that they learned to grow in abundance upon their land.

Bochica also taught the people about time. He explained that there was a right time for planting, a right time for harvesting, a time for the people to rejoice and celebrate, a time for hard work, a time to be born and a time to die as well. The bible of course contains the same teachings. Bochica taught the people about good conduct. They must, he explained, learn to work together, and they must be kind and generous to each other and to look after those in need.

"You needn't turn to the gods for everything," Bochica told the people. "You can care for yourselves." And so the people continued to praise their gods, but they no longer waited helplessly for whatever might come. Instead, they learned to build communities and to work together. And they loved their teacher, Bochica.

Bochica married a woman known as Huythaca, and for many years, he and his wife lived together happily. Like those around them, Bochica and Huythaca cared for each other. But as she grew older, Huythaca began to wish for more time and attention from her husband. She complained that he spent too much time taking care of others. She envied the commitment he felt toward the people.

"Stay with me," she begged when he set out to help the people till the soil. "Stay with me and let the others do the work themselves. You have done enough." But Bochica had taught the people about selflessness, about the importance of giving. He shook his head at his wife's request. "You must understand, this is the way people must live," he told her. "I must always be generous with the people."

"Be generous to me," Huythaca said. "I am your wife." But Bochica brushed away her words and paid no attention to his wife's growing unhappiness. He was a good person, but even good people don't always see clearly. Bochica did not notice that his wife's envy was turning to anger and bitterness. As the years passed, Huythaca's bitterness grew. She began to resent the people, and she dreamed of their destruction.

One day, when her seething fury had turned into a terrible fever, she walked to the river's edge. There she stood upon the banks and prayed. She prayed to Chibchacun, god of the waters. She prayed that he would stir the waters, that they would rise and flood the land, that even Bochica would be helpless to stop the destruction that would invade the land.

Resentful that Bochica had turned the people from the gods, Chibchacun heard Huythaca's prayer. And so he agreed to answer her prayers. He stirred the river, and the water began to rise.

The people, seeing the rising water, raced to save their animals and homes, but they were not quick enough. Soon the savannah was flooded, and with the spreading water, their homes and crops began to wash away. With the great chiefs at his side, Bochica strode to Tequendama. He was furious at his wife, and also furious with Chibchacun, but more than fury, determination fueled him. He would save the land and the people he loved. When he reached Tequendama, he climbed upon a rainbow. Standing above his people and above the flood, he tapped the rocks with his gold scepter. To the chiefs' astonishment, the waters parted, then, slipping into new paths, finding new ways to flow. And there, at Tequendama, a waterfall formed. The land was once again safe.

But when Bochica saw the devastation the flood had caused, his heart broke. He had saved the land, but many lives had already been lost.

Bochica grieved for those lost people as if they were his own children, and his anger toward his wife grew fiercer. That is when the people learned of Bochica's greatest powers, for he commanded that, from that day on, Chibchacun would carry the Earth upon his shoulders. And he commanded that his wife live upon the moon. To further insult his wife, he taught the people to live by a calendar based upon the movements of the sun. Ever since that day the moon, with Huythaca living on its surface, transits the sky. When people look up, they see Huythaca in her place in the heavens, and with this sight, they remember the destruction she once caused. And they remember, too, the importance of the Earth for their survival and well-being.

Still, after all these centuries, Huythaca remains bitter. Now and then she will, in anger, cause the waters of the Earth to swell and rise. The people understand they must never ignore her, and must take notice of both sun and moon whenever they are planting their fields.' (41) The author has not been able to find any information as regards when Bochica appeared in the area, but the fact that he did come from the east could, possibly infer that he was Viracochan or Quetzalcoatl. More data is required in order to establish if this is the case.

6/ Gucumatz

Possible depiction of Gucumatz at Placeres, Campeche, Mexico

We next move to the northwest and in fact connect with the Path of Viracocha in Central America. This creation myth comes from the Popul Vuh, the Quiché Maya book of creation. The Mayan gods create the natural world. Then, they try three times to create people who will praise them. On the third try, they succeed.

'There was a time when the world was empty. There were no people, no birds, no fish. There was only sky and sea. Two gods Tepeu, the Maker, and Gucumatz, the Feathered Spirit ruled this emptiness. After a time, the gods grew lonely. They decided to create the world.

They created light first. They simply thought the word "light," and light appeared. Next, the gods thought the word "earth." Immediately, land rose from the sea. They thought the words "mountain," "tree," "rock," and "lake." All these took shape.

"Creation of the Earth" by Diego Rivera

The gods were happy with their creation. But they still thought something was missing. They wanted to hear voices speak their names. They wanted to hear songs of praise. But rocks, trees, mountains, and lakes could not speak. Tepeu and Gucumatz conferred. They decided to make creatures to live on the land. Tepeu started first. He thought "bird," and birds of all types flew in the sky and perched in trees. He thought "deer," and deer grazed on the mountainsides. Then, Gucumatz thought "jaguar" and "snake," and these creatures appeared and lived in the jungle. And so it went until the gods had created all the animals. Then, Tepeu commanded the animals to speak. The animals made their sounds. The birds squawked. The jaguars growled. The snakes hissed. But these sounds were not words, and the gods were disappointed. They still wanted to hear voices praising their names. The two gods conferred. They decided to create people. They shaped the new creatures from wet clay. But these clay people were not right. They had no faces. They had no minds. They couldn't speak or think. Their bodies were lopsided and lumpy. When they tried to walk, their bodies crumbled and then fell apart.

The gods were disappointed again. They decided to destroy the clay people. They put them outside in the rain. Soon, the rain dissolved all of the clay people. Tepeu and Gucumatz decided to try again. This time, they carved people out of wood. The new people had faces. They could walk without crumbling or falling apart. But the wooden people were not right either. Their minds were empty. They couldn't think at all. Everything they said was nonsense. Everything they did was idiotic. Now, the gods were very frustrated. They called on Hurakán, the Heart of Heaven, the god of wind and storm. Hurakán sent a great flood. The waters rolled over the wooden people and drowned many of them. Then, the gods commanded the animals to attack and kill the survivors. A few of the survivors escaped from the animals and hid in the jungle. They became monkeys. Now, the gods knew that they couldn't make people out of wood or clay. However, they still wanted people who could speak and who could pray to them.

They conferred again. They decided to use corn to make new people. They ground the corn into a paste. From this paste, they shaped four men. These men were strong. They were smart. They had thoughts and feelings. And they could pray and praise the names of the gods. At first, the gods were very happy with the corn people. But then they noticed that the corn people were too perfect. They knew everything that the gods knew. They could see everything that the gods could see. The gods decided to change the corn people just a little bit. They made the corn people a little less intelligent. Now the corn people couldn't see, think, or speak as well as their creators. The corn people could still praise the gods' names, however. And they could still think, speak, and see well enough. Now, Tepeu, Gucumatz, and Hurakán were happy with their world, their creation. They made four corn women to marry the four corn men. The four corn couples built houses and cities. They had children, and their children had children. They were the ancestors of the Quiché Maya people.' (42)

Gucumatz, alternatively Qucumatz, Gukumatz, Gugumatz, Kucumatz etc. was a deity of the Post classic K'iche' Maya. He is considered to be the rough equivalent of the Aztec god Quetzalcoatl, and also of Kukulkan of the Yucatec or Yucatan Maya tradition. It is likely that the feathered serpent deity was borrowed from one of these two peoples and blended with other deities to provide the god Gucumatz that the K'iche' worshipped. (43) Gucumatz may have had his origin in the Valley of Mexico; some scholars have equated the deity with the Aztec deity Ehecatl-Quetzalcoatl, who was also a creator god. He may originally have been the same god as Tohil, the K'iche' sun god who also had attributes of the feathered serpent, but they later diverged and each deity came to have a separate priesthood. Gucumatz, god of wind and rain, was closely associated with Tepeu, god of lightning and fire. Both of these deities were considered to be the mythical ancestors of the K'iche' nobility by direct male line (44) but unlike Viracochan, for example, there appears to be no actual human counterpart.

Quetzal bird in the wild

The name translates literally as "Quetzal Serpent" although it is often rendered less accurately as "Feathered Serpent". The name derives from the K'iche' word q'uq, referring to the Resplendent quetzal Pharomachrus mocinno, a brightly coloured bird of the cloud forests of southern Mesoamerica. This is combined with the word kumatz "snake". The male Resplendent quetzal boasts iridescent blue-green tail feathers measuring up to 1 meter (3.3 ft) long that were prized by the Maya elite. The blue-green feathers symbolized vegetation and the sky, symbols of life for the ancient Maya, while the bright red feathers of the bird's chest symbolized fire. (45) Together, this combination gave a profound religious symbolism to the bird. The snake was a Maya symbol of rebirth due to its habit of shedding its skin to reveal a fresher one underneath. Gucumatz thus combined the celestial characteristics of the Quetzal with the serpentine underworld powers of the snake, giving him power over all levels of the Maya universe.

These characteristics also indicated a sexual duality between his masculine feathered serpent aspect and his feminine association with water and wind. This duality enabled the god to serve as a mediator between the masculine sun god Tohil and the feminine moon goddess Awilix, a role that was symbolised with the Mesoamerican ballgame. The Kaqchikel Maya were closely linked to the K'iche' and one of their ancestors, Gagavitz, was said to have thrown himself into Lake Atitlán and transformed himself into the deity, thus raising a storm upon the water and forming a whirlpool. (46) This is interesting in that unlike the Viracocha god creating his human counterpart Viracochan, Gagavitz, a human, transforms into a god.

Gucumatz was not directly equivalent to the Mexican Quetzalcoatl; he combined his attributes with those of the Classic Period Chontal Maya creator god Itzamna and was a two headed serpentine sky monster that carried the sun across the sky. Sculptures of a human face emerging between the jaws of a serpent were common from the end of the Classic Period through to the Late Post classic and may represent Gucumatz in the act of carrying Hunahpu, the youthful avatar of the sun god Tohil, across the sky. After midday, Gucumatz continued into the west and descended towards the underworld bearing an older sun. Such sculptures were used as markers for the Mesoamerican ballgame. (47) The site of Utatlan, which became the local Maya capital was founded by a king called Gucumatz around 1400 AD for its defensive position, however there is some disagreement as to whether he is a historical or a mythological figure. Utatlan is almost exactly on the Path of Viracocha, and relatively close to the Pacific Ocean.

7/ Votan

We now move slightly north to the ancient Maya center of Palenque. Votan, appearing as the bearded "god" clothed in a long, flowing robe, disembarked with his crew from a flotilla of ships upon the Gulf coast of Mexico. He then ascended the Usumacinta River and established Na-Chan (or Na-Kan), the "City of Serpents," tentatively identified as Palenque in Chiapas, Mexico. He is sometimes referred to as Lord Pacal, whose tomb was found in the Temple of the Inscriptions at Palenque.

Part of the lid of Lord Pacal's tomb in Palenque

However, this famous Mayan ruler, who reigned between 615 and 683 AD, may have merely assumed the name of the much earlier deity. (48) The lid of Pacal's sarcophagus gained pop culture status, by the way, when in the late 60's Erich von Daniken interpreted it as showing Pacal Votan seated at the control panel of an extraterrestrial spacecraft.

The actual name Votan comes from the Tzendal Maya of Chiapas. It literally means 'heart', and he was known as "the heart of the people." This deified human reputedly kept a record of the origin of the native races, which he gave to the guardians of a subterranean "Hall of Records" in Mesoamerica. The whereabouts of this depository are still unknown. John Van Auken of the Edgar Cayce Foundation provides compelling evidence that it may be located at Piedras Negras in Guatemala, though this remains unconfirmed. (49)

In the Mayan mythological, historical, medical, astrological, and esoteric text called Chilam Balam, for instance, we find the following prophetic lines: "Itzamná Kauil shall rise. Our lord comes, Itzá. Our elder brother comes, oh men of Tantun (Island of Cozumel). Receive your guests, the bearded men, the men of the east, the bearers of the sign of God, lord." (50) Votan was the archetypal bringer of civilization, bequeathing hieroglyphic writing, the codification of laws, the use of a complex Mesoamerican calendar, the cultivation of maize and cotton, sacrificial offerings of flowers and fruits rather than humans,

and su...
and me...

Lord Pacal's death outfit

The burial place of Pacal at Palenque

But where did he come from? According to some authorities, he may have been a Phoenician from Carthage (modern-day Tunis). Author Adrian Gilbert, for instance, believes that the evidence for this rests in the friezes at Palenque. He says that the figures depicted there have large noses and their facial features generally look Semitic. (51) Researcher Andrew Collins, on the other hand, thinks that Votan was probably a Hebrew, citing the Phoenicians' lack of serpent worship as well as their mercantile motives for navigation that superseded any interest in empire building. (52)

The story of Votan in Mexico dates back to at least the late 17th century. It was first published in Constituciones diocesanas del obispado de Chiappa (1702) by Francisco Núñez de la Vega, Bishop of Chiapas. According to Francisco Javier Clavijero:

'F. Núñez de la Vega, bishop of Chiapas, says, in the preface to his Synodal Constitutions, that in the visit which he made to his diocese towards the end of the last century (the late 1600s), he found many ancient calendars of the Chiapanese, and an old manuscript in the language of that country, made by the Indians themselves, in which it was said, according to their ancient tradition, that a certain person named Votan was present at that great building, which was made by order of his uncle, in order to mount up to heaven; that then every people was given its language, and that Votan himself was charged by God to make the division of the lands of Anahuac. The prelate adds afterwards, that there was in his time in Teopixca a great settlement of that diocese, a family of the surname of Votan, who were the reputed descendants of that ancient populator. We are not here endeavoring to give the antiquity to the populator of America on the faith of the Chiapanese, but merely to show that the Americans conceived themselves the descendants of Noah.' (53) Likely another example of the Catholic church twisting oral traditions to suit their needs.

In his account, Bishop Núñez de Vega also states that Votan belonged to the royal lineage of "Cham" (probably "chan" or snake) and that he established a kingdom called "Na Chan"

(Snake House) on the Usumacinta River that eventually extended across Chiapas and Soconusco to the Pacific Coast.

The author exploring possible megalithic elements at Palenque

Additional information can be found in a 1786 publication by Antonio del Río that cites the same sources as Clavigero and speculates at length on Votan's identity and travels to the Old World. As we have seen, there are references to Votan and perhaps his people being bearded, and having snake affiliations, but no actual Plumed Serpent descriptions have thus far been found.

8/ Itzamna

Colonial Izamal built on much earlier foundations

Slightly to the northeast of Palenque is the ancient center of Izamal, home of the deity known as Itzamna. He was one of the most important deities of Mayan mythology. The ruler of the heavens and of day and night, he was often shown in Mayan art as a pleasant, toothless old man with a large nose. He was also identified as the son of the creator god Hunab Ku. In various myths, Itzamna appears as a culture hero who gave the Maya the foundations of civilization. According to legend, he taught them to grow corn, to write, to use calendars, and to practice medicine. He also introduced a system for dividing up the land, and he established rituals for religious worship. (54)

Little is known about him, but scattered references are present in early colonial Spanish reports and dictionaries. Twentieth century Lacandon lore includes tales about a creator god (Nohochakyum or Hachakyum) who may be a late successor to Itzamna. In the pre-Spanish period, Itzamna, represented by the aged god D, was frequently depicted in books and in ceramic scenes derived from such books as possibly the famous Popul Vu. J. Eric S. Thompson originally interpreted the name Itzamna as "lizard house", itzam being a Yucatecan term for an iguana and naaj meaning "house". (55) However, Thompson's translation has gradually been abandoned. While there is no consensus on the exact meaning of the name Itzamna, it may be significant that "itz" is a root denoting all sorts of secretions (such as dew, sap, and semen) and also sorcery. The otherwise unattested, agentive form itzam could thus mean "asperser" or "sorcerer".

The early colonial sources variously connect, and sometimes identify, Itzamna with Hunab Ku (an invisible high god), Kinich Ahau (the sun deity), and Yaxcocahmut (a bird of omen).

The most reliable source on Itzamna, Diego de Landa, mentions him several times in the framework of his description of the ritual year. In the month of Uo, a ritual aspersion of the books took place under invocation of Kinich Ahau Itzamna, "the first priest." In the month of Zip, Itzamna was invoked as one of the gods of medicine, and in the month of Mac, he was venerated by the very old on a par with the Chaacs, the rain deities. In the cycle of four years, one year was under the patronage of Itzamna.

Carving of Itzamna in the Tonina site museum

He was also an active creator god, as is shown by the following. Confirming Landa's description of the book ritual above, Itzamna is stated by Diego López de Cogolludo to have invented the priestly art of writing. According to this same author, Itzamna (now written Zamna) had been a sort of priest who divided the land of Yucatán and assigned names to all of its features. More generally, Itzamna was the creator of humankind, and also the father of Bacab a fourfold deity of the interior of the earth. From the Late Postclassic Paris Codex back in time to the Pre-Classic San Bartolo murals, god D (Itzamna) has the so-called Principal Bird Deity for a transformative shape. The bird often holds a bicephalous snake in its beak. Its head sometimes resembles that of a rain deity; at other times, it is more like that of a bird of prey, perhaps the laughing falcon believed to be a harbinger of rain. (56)

There are apparently no references to him being bearded, and that his name refers to a god is clear, but whether he was also a human is unknown. As well, when he actually existed is unknown at this time.

9/ Kukulkan

The world famous "El Castillo" structure at Chichen Itza

Very close to Izamal and the center of Itzamna presence and worship is the world famous ancient site of Chichen Itza, center of the equally famous character known as Kukulkan, who was a Maya snake deity and also supposedly historical persons. Although heavily "Mexicanised," with Mexican being a name for the later Aztec people, Kukulkan has his origins among the Maya of the Classic Period, (200 AD to 1000) when he was known as Waxaklahun Ubah Kan, the War Serpent, and he has been identified as the Postclassic version of the Vision Serpent of Classic Maya art. (57) Although the "cult" of Kukulkan was originally centred on the ancient city of Chichén Itzá in the modern Mexican state of Yucatán, it spread as far as the

Guatemalan highlands. And some authors in fact believe that Kukulkan dates back to the Olmec period.

Author and classic Olmec head in the Mexico national museum

The Olmec are a civilization that first appears in a region of modern-day Mexico, along the Gulf of Mexico to the east of the Tuxtla Mountains around 1400 BC. Olmec culture peaked at around 900 BC and then gradually disappeared by 400 BC. The decline of Olmec civilization has not been fully explained, though environmental changes, possibly involving nearby volcanic activity, are likely to blame. Following their decline remaining Olmec population is likely to have lived in smaller communities in the area, or integrated with neighbouring civilizations.

Symbols of Olmec writing date back as far as 900 BC, suggesting that the Olmec may have had the earliest writing system of the Americas, though claims that this was a true writing system, and that it inspired the later Mayan script are disputed (there are claims that it was the Maya who first developed writing). The long-count calendar used by other civilizations, again most notably the Maya, may have been an Olmec invention, but this too is speculation.

Unlike the Maya and Aztec cultures, there is no surviving record of Olmec beliefs. What is known about Olmec mythology has been determined by studying Olmec art and inscriptions that did survive, and by comparing Olmec beliefs to other, later Mesoamerican cultures. (58) The name Olmec means "rubber people" in Nahuatl, the Aztec language. It was the Aztec name for the people who once lived in this area, and extracted latex from rubber trees. Europeans mistakenly assigned the name to ancient ruins that they found there, not realizing that those ruins pre-dated the Aztec and all other civilizations in the area. The word "Olmec" also refers to the rubber balls, used for the ancient ball game of Olmec creation. (59)

In Yucatán, references to the deity Kukulkan are confused by references to a named individual who bore the name of the god. Because of this, the distinction between the two has become blurred. This individual appears to have been a ruler or priest at Chichen Itza, who first appeared around the 10th century AD, however, he may have adopted the name from a much older person that may have existed around 200 AD. Although Kukulkan was mentioned as a historical person by Maya writers of the 16th century, the earlier 9th century texts at Chichen Itza never identified him as human and artistic representations depicted him as a Vision Serpent entwined around the figures of nobles. (60)

Feathered serpent representation at Chichen Itza

In the Yucatec language of Yucatan, the name is spelt K'uk'ulkan and in Tzotzil (Chiapas Mayan) it is K'uk'ul-chon. The Yucatec form of the name is formed from the word kuk (feather) with the adjectival suffix -ul, giving kukul (feathered), combined with can (snake), giving a literal meaning of "feathered snake".

Although the cult of Kukulkan had its origins in earlier Maya (or less likely Olmec) traditions, the Itza worship of Kukulkan was heavily influenced by the Quetzalcoatl "cult" of central Mexico. This influence probably arrived via Chontal Maya merchants from the Gulf Coast of Mexico. These Chontal merchants probably actively promoted the feathered serpent cult throughout Mesoamerica. Kukulkan headed a pantheon of deities of mixed Maya and non-Maya provenance, used to promote the Itza political and commercial agenda. It also eased the passage of Itza merchants into central Mexico and other non-Maya areas, promoting the Itza economy.

Another example of the feathered serpent at Chichen Itza

At Chichen Itza, Kukulkan ceased to be the Vision Serpent that served as a messenger between the king and the gods and came instead to symbolize the divinity of the state.

Spring equinox at Chichen Itza and shadow

The famous pyramidal structure commonly known as El Castillo in Chichen Itza served as a temple to Kukulkan. During the spring and fall equinoxes the shadow cast by the angle of the sun and edges of the nine steps of the pyramid combined with the northern stairway and the stone serpent head carvings create the illusion of a massive serpent descending the pyramid. After the fall of Chichen Itza, the nearby Postclassic city of Mayapan became the centre of the revived Kukulkan cult, with temples decorated with feathered serpent columns. (61) At the time of the Spanish Conquest, the high priest of Kukulkan was the family patriarch of the Xiu faction and was one of the two most powerful men in the city.

"According to Maya legend" the Maya were visited by a robed Caucasian man with blond hair, blue eyes and a beard by the name of Kukulkan who taught the Maya about agriculture, medicine, mathematics and astronomy. However, as far as the author can tell there are no academic sources that can back that up with up any hard evidence whatsoever.

10/ Quetzalcoatl

Several Quetzalcoatl heads at Teotihuacan

Quetzalcoatl's name comes from the Nahuatl (Aztec) language and means "feathered serpent". The worship of this feathered serpent is first known documented in the Teotihuacan area near Mexico in the first century BC or first century AD. That period lies within the Late Pre-classic to Early Classic period (400 BC to 600 AD) of Mesoamerican chronology, and veneration of the figure appears to have spread throughout Mesoamerica by the Late Classic (600–900 AD.) (62) In the Postclassic period (900 to 1519 AD), the worship of the feathered serpent deity was based in the primary Mexican religious center of Cholula. It is in this period that the deity known to have been named "Quetzalcoatl" by his Nahua followers came to its greatest prominence.

A small part of the massive ruins at Cholula

In the era following the 16th century Spanish Conquest, a number of texts were written that conflate Quetzalcoatl with Ce Acatl Topiltzin, a ruler of the mythico-historic city of Tollan. Tollan is the name given to the mythical place of origin in many Mesoamerican traditions, including those of the Aztecs and the K'iche' Maya. In the K'iche' epic Popul Vuh, the first people created are gathered at Tollan, the place of seven caves, where they receive their languages and their gods. It is a matter of much debate among historians to which degree, or whether at all, these narratives about this legendary Toltec ruler describe historical events. (63) Furthermore, early Spanish sources written by clerics tend to identify the god ruler Quetzalcoatl of these narratives with either conquistador Hernán Cortés or St. Thomas. However, as we have seen earlier, the Spanish used oral traditions of those they conquered and warped them for their own dark purposes.

Among the Aztec, whose beliefs are the best documented in the historical sources, Quetzalcoatl was related to gods of the wind, of the planet Venus, of the dawn, of merchants and of arts, crafts and knowledge. He was also the patron god of the Aztec priesthood, of learning and knowledge. Quetzalcoatl was one of several important gods in the Aztec pantheon, along with the gods Tlaloc, Tezcatlipoca and Huitzilopochtli. Two other gods represented by the planet Venus are Quetzalcoatl's ally Tlaloc who is the god of rain, and Quetzalcoatl's twin who is named Xolotl, the god of fire and lighting, sickness and deformities.

The author with a massive ancient Tlaloc sculpture in Mexico City

The first culture to use the symbol of a feathered serpent as an important religious and political symbol was Teotihuacan. At temples such as the aptly named "Quetzalcoatl temple" in the Ciudadela complex, feathered serpents figure prominently and alternate with a different kind of serpent head. The earliest depictions of the feathered serpent deity were fully zoomorphic, depicting the serpent as an actual snake, but already among the Classic Maya the deity began acquiring human features. Teotihuacan is located on the outskirts of Mexico City, and when we look at the map of the east coast of the Americas we can see that the Path of Viracocha goes almost straight through this area. Coincidence?

View of the Temple of the Sun from the Temple of the Moon

The archaeological record shows that after the fall of Teotihuacan that marked the beginning of the epi-classic period in Mesoamerican chronology around 600 AD, the "cult" of the feathered serpent spread to the new religious and political centers in central Mexico, centers such as Xochicalco, Cacaxtla and Cholula. These places are less than 2 hours' drive from Mexico City and thus still very close to the Path of Viracocha.

Quetzalcoatl carving at Xochicalco

Feathered serpent iconography is prominent at all of these sites. Cholula is known to have remained the most important center of worship to Quetzalcoatl, the Aztec/Nahua version of the feathered serpent deity, in the post-classic period. In the post-classic Nahua civilization of central Mexico (Aztec), the worship of Quetzalcoatl was ubiquitous. The most important center was Cholula where the world's largest pyramid was dedicated to his worship. In Aztec culture, depictions of Quetzalcoatl were fully anthropomorphic.

A small portion of the massive Cholula pyramidal structure

On the basis of the Teotihuacan iconographical depictions of the feathered serpent, archaeologist Karl Taube has argued that the feathered serpent was a symbol of fertility and internal political structures contrasting with the War Serpent symbolizing the outward military expansion of the Teotihuacan civilization. (64) Historian Enrique Florescano also analyzing Teotihuacan iconography argues that the Feathered Serpent was part of a triad of agricultural deities: The Goddess of the Cave symbolizing motherhood, reproduction and life, Tlaloc, god of rain, lightning and thunder and the feathered serpent, god of vegetation renewal. The feathered serpent was furthermore connected to the planet Venus because of this planet's importance as a sign of the beginning of the rainy season.

Many feathered serpent heads at the Quetzalcoatl temple at Teotihuacan

To the Aztecs, Quetzalcoatl was, as his name indicates, a feathered serpent, a flying reptile (much like a dragon), who was a boundary-maker (and transgressor) between earth and sky. He was a creator deity having contributed essentially to the creation of Mankind. He also had anthropomorphic forms, for example in his aspects as Ehecatl the wind god. Among the

Aztecs, the name Quetzalcoatl was also a priestly title, as the two most important priests of the Aztec Templo Mayor were called "Quetzalcoatl Tlamacazqui". In the Aztec ritual calendar, different deities were associated with the cycle-of-year names: Quetzalcoatl was tied to the year Ce Acatl (One Reed), which correlates to the year 1519. (65) This was also the year when Hernan Cortes invaded Mexico.

Since the sixteenth century, it has been widely held that the Aztec Emperor Moctezuma II initially believed the landing of Hernan Cortes in 1519 to be Quetzalcoatl's return. This view has been questioned by ethno-historians who argue that the Quetzalcoatl-Cortes connection is not found in any document that was created independently of post-Conquest Spanish influence, and that there is little proof of a pre-Hispanic belief in Quetzalcoatl's return. (66)

Tula warriors with snake headband and feathers

Most documents expounding this theory are of entirely Spanish origin, such as Cortes's letters to Charles V of Spain, in which Cortes goes to great pains to present the naive gullibility of the Aztecs in general as a great aid in his conquest of Mexico. Such arrogance and complete misunderstanding of native people is appalling. Much of the idea of Cortes' being seen as a deity can be traced back to the Florentine Codex written down some 50 years after the conquest. In the Codex's description of the first meeting between Moctezuma and Cortes, the Aztec ruler is described as giving a prepared speech in classical oratorial

Nahuatl, a speech which, as described in the codex written by the Franciscan Bernardino de Sahagún and his Tlatelolcan informants, included such prostrate declarations of divine or near-divine admiration as:

'You have graciously come on earth, you have graciously approached your water, your high place of Mexico, you have come down to your mat, your throne, which I have briefly kept for you, I who used to keep it for you.'

and:

'You have graciously arrived, you have known pain, you have known weariness, now come on earth, take your rest, enter into your palace, rest your limbs; may our lords come on earth.'

Some scholarship still maintains the view that the Aztec Empire's fall may be attributed in part to the belief in Cortes as the returning Quetzalcoatl. However, a majority of modern Mesoamericanist scholars consider the "Quetzalcoatl/Cortes myth" as one of many myths about the Spanish conquest which have risen in the early post-conquest period.

While there is no question that the legend of Quetzalcoatl played a significant role in colonial period accounts of the conquest, a 2012 exhibition at the Los Angeles County Museum of Art and the Dallas Museum of Art and funded by the National Endowment for the Humanities, "The Children of the Plumed Serpent: the Legacy of Quetzalcoatl in Ancient Mexico" conceived by John Pohl and curated with Virginia Fields and

Victoria Lyall demonstrated the existence of a powerful confederacy of Eastern Nahua, Mixtec and Zapotec, along with the peoples they dominated throughout southern Mexico between 1200 to 1600.

Possible depiction of an ancient bearded man in the Mexico Anthropology Museum

They maintained a major pilgrimage and commercial center at Cholula, Puebla which the Spaniards compared to both Rome and Mecca because the cult of the god united its constituents through a field of common social, political, and religious values without dominating them militarily. This confederacy engaged in almost seventy-five years of nearly continuous conflict with the Aztec of the Triple Alliance until the arrival of Cortes at which time a number of factions throughout Tlaxcala, Puebla, and Oaxaca provided the Spaniards with the army that first reclaimed the city of Cholula from its pro-Aztec ruling faction, and ultimately defeated the Aztec capital of Tenochtitlan (Mexico City). The Tlaxcalteca along with other city states across the Plain of Puebla then supplied the auxiliary and logistical support for the conquests of Guatemala and West Mexico while Mixtec and Zapotec caciques (Colonial indigenous rulers) gained monopolies in the overland transport of Manila galleon trade through Mexico, and formed highly lucrative relationships with the Dominican order in the new Spanish imperial world economic system that explains so much of the enduring legacy of indigenous life ways that characterize southern Mexico and explain the popularity of the Quetzalcoatl legends that continued through the colonial period to the present day.

Hernan Cortes

11/ Pahana and Awanyu

From the Valley of Mexico if we follow the Path of Viracocha we reach the Hopi reservation in Arizona. The Hopi maintain a complex religious and mythological tradition stretching back over centuries. However, it is difficult to definitively state what all Hopis as a group believe. Like the oral traditions of many other societies, Hopi mythology is not always told consistently and each Hopi mesa, or even each village, may have its own version of a particular story. But, "in essence the variants of the Hopi myth bear marked similarity to one another." (67)

It is also not clear that those stories which are told to non-Hopis, such as anthropologists and ethnographers, represent genuine Hopi beliefs or are merely stories told to the curious while keeping safe the Hopi's more sacred doctrines. As folklorist Harold Courlander states, "there is a Hopi reticence about discussing matters that could be considered ritual secrets or religion-oriented traditions." The Hopi had at least some contact with Europeans beginning the 16th century, and some believe that European Christian traditions may have entered into Hopi cosmology at some point. Indeed, Spanish missions were built in several Hopi villages starting in 1629 and were in operation until the Pueblo Revolt of 1680. However, after the revolt, it was the Hopi alone of all the Pueblo tribes who kept the Spanish out of their villages permanently, and regular contact with whites did not begin again until nearly two centuries later. The Hopi mesas have therefore been seen as "relatively unacculturated" at least through the early twentieth century, and it may be posited that the European influence on the core themes of Hopi mythology was slight. (68)

The true Pahana (or Bahana) is the Lost White Brother of the Hopi. Most versions have it that the Pahana or Elder Brother left for the east at the time that the Hopi entered the Fourth World and began their migrations. However, the Hopi say that he will return again and at his coming the wicked will be destroyed and a new age of peace, the Fifth World, will be ushered into the world. Traditionally, Hopis are buried facing eastward in expectation of the Pahana who will come from that direction. (69)

The legend of the Pahana seems intimately connected with the Aztec story of Quetzalcoatl, and other legends of Central America. This similarity is furthered by the liberal representation of Awanyu, the horned or plumed serpent, in Hopi and other Puebloan art. This figure bears a striking resemblance to figures of Quetzacoatl, the feathered serpent, in Mexico. In the early 16th century, both the Hopis and the Aztecs believed that the coming of the Spanish conquistadors was the return of this lost white prophet. Or was this a story in fact made up by the Spanish themselves? Unlike the Aztecs, upon first contact the Hopi put the Spanish through a series of tests in order to determine their divinity, and having failed, the Spanish were sent away from the Hopi mesas. (70)

For more than a millennium, the horned or plumed serpent, known in the Tewa Pueblo (Hopi) language as Awanyu, has occupied a place of great importance within the culture and cosmology of the Puebloan Indians of the American Southwest. Symbolic both of earthly and supernatural phenomena; clouds, rain, lightning, bodies of water and the fusion of the terrestrial to the heavenly its likeness has snaked itself across the steep desert rock faces and sheer cliff overhangs over thousands of miles of the temperamental desert terrain within the vast radius of what now constitutes the territories of Mexico, New Mexico, Arizona and Colorado. (71) Archaeologist Polly Schaafsma, Ph.D., is well acquainted with Awanyu, having dedicated many years of study to its mysterious and powerful presence throughout the Southwest. In an essay "Quetzalcoatl and the Horned and Feathered Serpent of the Southwest" (found in the book The Road To Aztlan: Art From A Mythic Homeland by Virginia M. Fields and Victor Zamudio-Taylor, 2001), she notes Awanyu's "bewilderingly complex personality," which, much like its Mexican counterpart, Quetzalcoatl, "is multifaceted and ambiguous, cosmic in scope, its roles in myth and ritual involving the unpredictable endings and beginnings, change, transition, and transformation."

Though the iconic symbol of the plumed or horned serpent is still used extensively among contemporary Pueblo artists, the secrets of Awanyu remain closely guarded; many sources are reluctant to offer dialogue on the subject of Awanyu, and therefore, the discourse is limited.

Beyond this point, at least as regards the Path of Viracocha and its relationship with light skinned teachers and Plumed Serpents the trail runs cold. There is an earth energy line actually called the Plumed Serpent which runs through the whole area we have been discussing, first learned about by the author from researcher Hugh Newman.

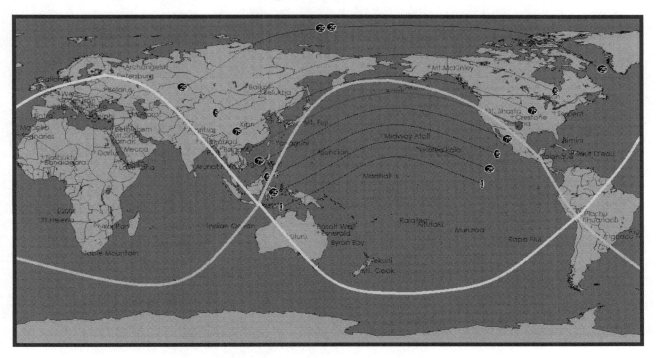

Plumed serpent or dragon energy line in yellow

It does correlate well with the path of Viracocha that we have been discussing, and we have seen that almost all of the locations that we have explored are on or near this line. Is it possible that there was a person or people who first appeared in the Lake Titicaca area of Bolivia around 100 AD and proceeded to follow this energy line over the course of a lifetime or possibly lifetimes in order to teach those that he/they encountered?

The Spanish conquerors of course used the oral traditions of the people they encountered and subsequently destroyed in many cases in order to attempt to convince them that they were the return of the great teachers. This book has simply been a preliminary study of the topic, and future travel and research will be carried out by the author in order to see if there truly were arrivals or an arrival of non-indigenous in the Americas prior to Columbus or indeed the Vikings.

The common theme of an arrival from the east, and departure to the west (or northwest) could indicate that they or he would have come from the Atlantic side of the planet, but no precise homeland has yet been made clear.

17/ Bibliography

1/ https://books.google.com.pe/books?id=0osWcOoQGf4C&pg=PA254&dq=white+gods&hl=en&ei=gpb3TYikLtCt8QOVnvjKCw&sa=X&oi=book_result&ct=result#v=onepage&q=white%20gods&f=false

2/ Pre-Columbian America: Myths and Legends, Donald. A. Mackenzie, Senate, 1996, p.268-270

3/ Rupert Furneaux, Ancient Mysteries, Ballantine Books, 1987, p. 154

4/ Braghine, The Shadow of Atlantis, p. 34

5/ Robert Marx, in quest of the great white gods: contact between the Old and New World from the dawn of history, Crown, 1992

6/ https://books.google.com.pe/books?id=uDTUF3wHlkoC&pg=PA65&dq=white+gods+harold+wilkins&hl=en&ei=5qj3TbLCCYbF8QPB65TeCw&sa=X&oi=book_result&ct=book-preview-link&redir_esc=y#v=onepage&q&f=false

7/ Nicholas Goodrick-Clarke, Black Sun: Aryan Cults, Esoteric Nazism, and the Politics of Identity, 2003 p. 81

8/ Wirth, Diane E. (2002), "Quetzalcoatl, the Maya maize god and Jesus Christ", Journal of Book of Mormon Studies (Provo, Utah: Maxwell Institute) 11 (1): 4–15

9/ Peter Kolosimo, Timeless Earth, 1977 pp. 153 - 154 ISBN 0-7221-5329-5

10/ The Oxford Encyclopedia of Mesoamerican Culture

11/ Pool, Christopher A. (2007). Olmec Archaeology and Early Mesoamerica. Cambridge World Archaeology. Cambridge and New York: Cambridge University Press. ISBN 978-0-521-78882-3.

12/ Covarrubias, Miguel (1957). Indian Art of Mexico and Central America (Color plates and line drawings by the author ed.). New York: Alfred A. Knopf.

13/ Castro, Ruben Cabrera (1993) "Human Sacrifice at the Temple of the Feathered Serpent: Recent Discoveries at Teotihuacan" Kathleen Berrin, Esther Pasztory, eds., Teotihuacan, Art from the City of the Gods, Thames and Hudson, Fine Arts Museums of San Francisco, ISBN 0-500-27767-2.

14/ Christenson, Allen (2007). Popol Vuh: The Sacred Book of the Maya. University of Oklahoma Press. ISBN 978-0-8061-3839-8. ISBN 0-8061-3839-4.

15/ http://www.sfu.museum/hola/en/slides/featured/42/

16/ http://www.whats-your-sign.com/snake-symbolic-meaning.html

17/ Mills, Alice; Parker, Janet & Stanton, Julie (2006). Mythology: Myths, Legends and Fantasies. New Holland Publishers. p. 493. ISBN 1-77007-453-8.

18/ https://en.wikipedia.org/wiki/Coat_of_arms_of_Mexico

19/ Ancient Mexico, Editorial Milenio

20/ http://www.behindthename.com/name/tenoch/submitted

21/ Dover, Robert V. H.; Katharine E. Seibold; John Holmes McDowell (1992). Andean cosmologies through time: persistence and emergence. Caribbean and Latin American studies. Indiana University Press. p. 274. ISBN 0-253-31815-7

22/ "Viracocha". Bloomsbury Dictionary of Myth. Bloomsbury Publishing Ltd., London. 1996

23/ "Viracocha". Bloomsbury Dictionary of Myth. Bloomsbury Publishing Ltd., London. 1996

24/ http://www.atlantisbolivia.org/atlantisoriginsinlegends.htm

25/ http://www.atlantisbolivia.org/atlantisoriginsinlegends.htm

26/ Viracocha and the Coming of the Incas from "History of the Incas" by Pedro Sarmiento De Gamboa, translated by Clements Markham, Cambridge: The Hakluyt Society 1907, pp. 28-58

27/ Pre-Columbian America: Myths and Legends, Donald. A. Mackenzie, Senate, 1996, p.268-270

28/ Anales de Cuauhtitlan., 1975, 9.

29/ http://weber.ucsd.edu/~dkjordan/nahuatl/ReadingQuetzalcoatl.html

30/ In Quest of the Great White Gods, Robert F. Marx, Crown Publishers, 1992 pp. 7-15

31/ "Dominquez and Escalante Expedition, 1776". UintahBasintah.org.

32/ Jones, Paul J (2009) author and travel writer, Peru Guide (the only), the online guide to Peru.

33/ http://ancientexplorers.com/blog/ancient-alignment-in-the-andes-hints-at-lost-global-high-culture/

34/ Sholten D'Ebneth, Maria, La Ruta de Wiracocha, Editorial Juan Mejía Baca, Lima, 1977

35/ Lajo, Javier, Qhapaq Ñan: La Ruta Inca de Sabiduría, Centro de Estudios Nueva Economía y Sociedad, Lima, 2005.

36/ Fernandez-Baca Tupayachi, Carlos, Saqsaywaman: A Model of Atlantis, the Untold Story, Munaypacha, Lima, 2006, p161

37/ Schoch, Robert M, Forgotten Civilization: the Role of Solar Outbursts in our Past and Future, Inner Traditions, Rochester Vermont, 2012

38/ Silverberg, Robert (1996) [1967]. The Golden Dream: Seekers of El Dorado. Ohio University Press. pp. 98–99. ISBN 0-8214-1170-5

39/ Paul Herrmann, Michael Bullock (1954). Conquest by Man. Harper & Brothers. p. 186. OCLC 41501509

40/ Arthur Flagg Cotterell (1986). A Dictionary of World Mythology. Oxford University Press. p. 204. ISBN 0-19-217747-8

41/ http://www.uexpress.com/tell-me-a-story/2004/10/17/bochica-and-the-flood-a-south

42/ file:///C:/Users/Brien/Downloads/Story.pdf

43/ Read, Kay Almere; Jason González (2000). Handbook of Mesoamerican Mythology. Oxford: ABC-CLIO. ISBN 1-85109-340-0

44/ Carmack, Robert M. (2001a). Kik'ulmatajem le K'iche'aab': Evolución del Reino K'iche' (in Spanish). Guatemala: Iximulew. ISBN 99922-56-22-2

45/ Christenson, Allen J. (2007) [2003]. "Popul Vuh: Sacred Book of the Quiché Maya People" (PDF online publication)

46/ Christenson, Allen J. (2007) [2003]. "Popul Vuh: Sacred Book of the Quiché Maya People" (PDF online publication)

47/ Fox, John W. (2008) [1987]. Maya Post classic state formation. Cambridge, UK and New York, USA: Cambridge University Press. ISBN 978-0-521-10195-0

48/ http://www.viewzone.com/votanx.html

49/ John Van Auken and Lora Little, The Lost Hall of Records: Edgar Cayce's Forgotten Record of the Human History in the Ancient Yucatan (Memphis, Tennessee: Eagle Wing Books, Inc., 2000)

50/ Book of the Chilam Balam, XXIV, translated by Ralph L. Roys, 1933, at www.sacred-texts.com

51/ Adrian Gilbert, Maurice M Cotterell, The Mayan Prophecies: Unlocking the Secrets of a Lost Civilization (Shaftesbury, Dorset: Element Books Limited, 1996, 1995), p. 202.

52/ Andrew Collins, introduction by David Rohl, Gateway to Atlantis (New York: Graf Publishers, Inc., 2000), p. 340.

53/ Clavigero, Francesco Saverio (1787). The history of Mexico. Collected from Spanish and Mexican historians, from manuscripts, and ancient paintings of the Indians. Illustrated by charts, and other copper plates. To which are added, critical dissertations on the land, the animals, and inhabitants of Mexico. By Abbé D. Francesco Saverio Clavigero., 2 vols. Translated from the original Italian, by Charles Cullen, Esq. London: G. G. J. and J. Robinson. OCLC 2671015

54/ http://www.encyclopedia.com/topic/Itzamna.aspx

55/ Eric Thompson, Maya History and Religion. Norman 1970

56/ Karen Bassie-Sweet, Maya Sacred Geography and the Creator Deities. Norman 2008

57/ Freidel, David A.; Linda Schele; Joy Parker (1993). Maya Cosmos: Three Thousand Years on the Shaman's Path. New York: William Morrow & Co. ISBN 0-688-10081-3. OCLC 27430287

58/ http://www.ancient-mythology.com/olmec/

59/ http://realhistoryww.com/world_history/ancient/Olmec_the_Americas.htm

60/ Freidel, David A.; Linda Schele; Joy Parker (1993). Maya Cosmos: Three Thousand Years on the Shaman's Path. New

York: William Morrow & Co. ISBN 0-688-10081-3. OCLC 27430287

61/ Sharer, Robert J.; Loa P. Traxler (2006). The Ancient Maya (6th (fully revised) ed.). Stanford, CA: Stanford University Press. ISBN 0-8047-4817-9. OCLC 57577446

62/ Ringle, William M.; Tomás Gallareta Negrón; George J. Bey (1998). "The Return of Quetzalcoatl". Ancient Mesoamerica (Cambridge University Press) 9 (2): 183–232

63/ Nicholson, H.B. (2001). The "Return of Quetzalcoatl": did it play a role in the conquest of Mexico?. Lancaster, CA: Labyrinthos

64/ Florescano, Enrique (1999). The Myth of Quetzalcoatl. Lysa Hochroth (trans.), Raúl Velázquez (illus.) (translation of El mito de Quetzalcóatl original Spanish-language ed.). Baltimore, MD: Johns Hopkins University Press. ISBN 0-8018-7101-8

65/ Townsend, Camilla (2003). "Burying the White Gods: New perspectives on the Conquest of Mexico". The American Historical Review 108 (3)

66/ Restall, Matthew (2003). Seven Myths of the Spanish Conquest. Oxford and New York: Oxford University Press. ISBN 0-19-516077-0

67/ Christopher Vecsey. The Emergence of the Hopi People, in American Indian Quarterly, vol. 7, no. 3, American Indian Religions, 70 (Summer 1983)

68/ David Roberts. The Pueblo Revolt, 5 (Simon and Schuster, 2004)

69/ Courlander, Harold, The Fourth World of the Hopis: The Epic Story of the Hopi Indians as Preserved in Their Legends and Traditions (University of New Mexico Press, 1987) page 31

70/ Raymond Friday Locke. The Book of the Navajo, 139-140 (Hollaway House 2001)

71/http://www.santafenewmexican.com/magazines/bienvenidos_2014/avanyu-spirit-of-water-in-pueblo-life-and-art/article_da0e9cb8-d4b2-11e3-9331-0017a43b2370.html

Made in United States
Troutdale, OR
08/02/2024

21698232R00066